Arnulfo L. Oliveira Memorial Library

Gloria Steinem

Doing Sixty & Seventy

 Elders Academy Press

Doing Sixty & Seventy is sponsored by AgeSong Senior Communities and published by Elders Academy Press, a program of Pacific Institute. Pacific Institute teaches new perspectives on aging in the field of gerontology and aims to reestablish the role of eldership in our society. The Institute is a nonprofit educational corporation that promotes individual and community wellness and helps advance, disseminate, and preserve knowledge in gerontological fields that focus on clinical, educational and human services purposes. www.pacificinstitute.org

Elders Academy Press seeks to help change perceptions of the elderly and aging and develop a vision of a contemporary Elder. The Press also seeks to encourage people to approach the process of aging with consciousness and to direct their thoughts toward possibilities ahead.

Elders Academy Press
432 Ivy Street
San Francisco, California 94102
www.elderspress.org

First Edition

Printed in the United States
Distributed to the book trade by Publishers Group West

Jacket + Interior Design Emily Tanner, www.emilytanner.com
Editing Leslie K. Lewis and Steve Boga
Founding Publisher Nader R. Shabahangi, Ph.D.
Managing Publisher Leslie K. Lewis + Doris Bersing, Ph.D.

Elders Academy Press' publications are available through most bookstores. Substantial discounts on bulk quantities are available to corporations, professional associations, and other organizations. Email books@pacificinstitute.org for details and discount information.

Library of Congress Cataloging-in-Publication Data
Steinem, Gloria.
 Doing Sixty and Seventy / by Gloria Steinem.—1st ed.
  p. cm.
Updated version of the author's essay Doing Sixty, originally published in 1994 as part of a larger collection of essays entitled *Moving Beyond Words*.
"Sponsored by AgeSong Senior Communities."
Includes bibliographical references and index.
ISBN-13: 978-0-9758744-2-4 (hardcover: alk. paper)
ISBN-10: 0-9758744-2-X
1. Older women. 2. Aging. 3. Ageism. 4. Self-realization in women. 5. Self-realization in old age.
I. Steinem, Gloria. Doing sixty. II. Title.
HQ1061.S74 2006
305.26'2—dc22
                    2006020073

table of contents

publisher's note

When reading *Doing Sixty*, by Gloria Steinem, I was mesmerized. It seemed to me that this thought-provoking, inspiring essay deserved more attention than it received when first published as part of a larger book of essays by Steinem.

It was this belief that led me to ask Ms. Steinem if Elders Academy Press could publish the essay as an independent volume. She graciously gave her permission, time in revising the essay and writing a Preface, and attended a publishing party.

Among other things, *Doing Sixty* explains Steinem's poignant views on age stereotyping, the unexpected liberation that comes with growing older, and defines what Steinem perceives as the fact that women become more radical as they age. Steinem describes her personal journey of turning fifty as "leaving a much-loved and familiar country" and turning sixty "as arriving at the border of a new one" in which she looked forward to "trading moderation for excess, defiance for openness, and planning of the unknown."

Readers will want to cheer at Steinem's statement that "I've come to realize the pleasures of being a nothing-to-lose, take-no-shit older woman; of looking at what once seemed to be outer limits but turned out to be just road signs." Steinem's attitude toward aging is simply inspirational. It provides reassurance and validation as well as impetus for continued growth and change.

Her conclusion that "More and more, there is only the full, glorious, alive-in-the-moment, don't-give-a-damn-yet-caring-for-everything sense of the right now" are spirited words to live by.

Her reflective insights in the essay also shed light on the forces that shaped her life—for readers who have only heard bits and pieces about her, the essay offers a primer on Steinem's bold and logical theories.

The Preface, written when Steinem is just past seventy and twelve years after the essay was first published, describes Steinem's development of her precious sense of mortality and time.

In that fabled list of five people you would like to meet in your life—Gloria Steinem tops my list. I have long admired the work she has done in her life and her writing and commentary about issues of gender, race, aging and other social movements. As such, this publishing project—an opportunity to publish the writing of one of the principal role models in my life—has been an extraordinary gift. It gives me great honor to think that Elders Academy Press and I have helped increase the opportunities for people to read Gloria Steinem's work.

Gloria Steinem became a spokesperson for issues about aging quite accidentally after declaring to a reporter on the occasion of her fortieth birthday, "This is what forty looks like. We've been lying for so long, who would know?" Because of this casual comment about her age and about the collective societal pressure to lie about our age she received an avalanche of thanks and support from other women facing age discrimination. This caused her to realize the far reaching dimensions of age oppression.

Ms. Steinem remains the United States' most influential, eloquent and revered feminist more than three decades after founding *Ms.* magazine. A devoted activist and writer, Steinem continues, as she has for more than thirty-five years, to travel nationally and internationally and speak with a calm voice of reason and articulation about gender, race, age, and other civil inequity issues.

Gloria Steinem is also quite funny. At an event we sponsored in December of 2004, Gloria Steinem brought down the house when she said, "One day I woke up and there was a seventy-year-old woman in my bed." The smile on her face, the spark in her eyes and her own ensuing hearty laughter said that this is a woman in love with life who doesn't take herself seriously—though, we know she takes social inequities such as age discrimination quite seriously. It is also obvious that she makes the best out of aging.

I hope you will enjoy Ms. Steinem's writing as much as I have.

Elders Academy Press would like to thank Susan Adelman, the Lucy and Isadore B. Adelman Foundation, Patri Merker Architects, Mackenzie Green, Natasha Boissier, Eleanor Coppola, LCSW, Antje Farber, Tonie Fowler, Terri Gill, Darlene

Hanggi, Karen Kortie, Kristina Kordesch, Ernest L. Lewis, Katie Mc Gonigal, Beth MacLeod, LCSW, Nancy L. Peterson, Mary Renner, Leda Sanford, Danan Barrett Sherman, Diane Westlake, Donna M. Williams, and the late Piero Patri for their generous support of this publishing project.

Personally, I would like to thank Doris Bersing, Ph.D., Nader Shabahangi, Ph.D., Steven Boga, and Emily Tanner for their help in developing and completing this project.

Leslie K. Lewis
Managing Publisher

preface

Into the seventies

Updating "Doing Sixty" almost a dozen years later is a way of talking with a previous self. Though I've had lessons since then in how utterly unpredictable life is, it's also a chance to give a nudge to the future. Indeed, I wish I'd taken stock this way at a younger age—sort of a metaphysical version of cleaning for company, then wishing you'd done it before—but this feels especially crucial now that I know more everyday, yet come ever closer to the unknown.

Even mentioning the unknown is a change. Well into my fifties, I had ignored aging in a way that was great for activism. At sixty, I was thinking about aging and leaving the center of life. At just past seventy, I'm conscious of the time I have before leaving it altogether; not at all the same thing. Even if I live to be a hundred, as I have every intention of doing, I will have less than thirty years to go: the same time I spent working on Ms. magazine, fewer years than I've lived in my current apartment, and about the same time I've been wearing my favorite pair of blue jeans.

To put this another way, aging feels like a process of the body, the concrete, the comparable, the mind. Making death real for even a millisecond feels like a mystery of the heart.

I'm not presuming that my experience is the same as yours. Everything that makes us unique—belief, culture, health, companionship, economics, hope, heredity—creates different paths on this universal journey. What I say here may be really helpful or really not. But I do have infinite faith in talking to each other. After all, we are communal creatures who must mirror each other to know who we are. Every living thing ages and dies, yet humans seem to be the only species that *thinks* about aging and *thinks* about dying. Surely, we are meant to use this ability, especially in a country that suffers so much from concealing aging and dying as if they were the last obscenities.

In retrospect, I realize that I, too, was in the Olympics of denial, yet some part of me needed to know the stages of life. Perhaps because I switched roles early and became the caretaker of my loving and sad mother, or because I didn't measure time by the usual periods of marriage, parenthood and the kind of career you retire from; perhaps because I didn't see a death early in my small family, or because I got so good at escaping into books and imaginary futures—for all these reasons, the central years of adulthood seemed as if they could stretch on forever. If I was "old" when I was young, and, according to work and lifestyle, "young" when I was old, how relevant could aging be?

If I couldn't get to aging, I certainly couldn't get to death. I used to joke that I thought I was immortal and this caused me to plan poorly. Of course, part of me knew this was no joke. Now that distance allows me to see patterns, I notice that I've always been trying to figure out these secrets.

At twenty-five or so when I came to New York to be a writer, I fell in love with Muriel Spark's *Memento Mori,* a little gem of a novel about a group of friends in London who are all connected by careers, marriages and affairs. Because they are now over seventy, gossip that once focused on work or sex has centered on who is losing which faculty. Each person has specific fears about aging and death, so we watch as each fearful imagining comes true.

I bought copies to give to my friends because I knew we had something to learn here. The message begins when a threatening phone caller announces to one character at a time, "Remember, you must die." Most of the friends respond with fear, outrage, even calls to Scotland Yard, but there are two exceptions. A woman novelist, disdained by the group because she is barely able to remember if she had her tea, yet envied because her writing is being rediscovered by a new generation of readers, infuriates her friends even more by insisting that *her* caller was, "a very civil young man." For the first time, we realize the various voices were each friend's personification of Death.

Then there is a retired inspector, asked by his friends to help find this caller or group of callers, who delivers the message: "If I had my life over again, I should form the habit of nightly composing myself to thoughts of death. I would practice, as it were, the remembrance of death. There is no other practice which so intensifies life. Death, when it approaches, ought not to take one by surprise. It should be part of the full expectation of life. Without an ever-present sense of death, life is insipid. You might as well live on the whites of eggs."[1]

I wanted to be exactly like the inspector or the novelist.

Before I was thirty, I was proposing *The Old Lady Book,* a collection of interviews with elderly women who seemed to know this secret of intensified life. You won't be surprised to learn that old ladies weren't considered commercial in the publishing world. Then I wrote an outline for *The Death Book,* an anthology of famous and not-so-famous last words and death scenes of men and women, real and fictional, sudden and lingering, from newspapers, novels, history, art and the comics. The idea was that, by the time the readers and I got to the end, we would be purged of denial, and able to see death as a social event. Needless to say, this was even less saleable.

No editor asked me—nor did I ask myself—why I was so interested in the end of life when I was so near its beginning. I didn't understand that we write what we need to know.

But there were other clues. For instance: I found old people more touching than children, an oddity in my generation when all women were supposed to be magnetized by all children. I was partly seeing the lost talents of my mother when I looked at aging female bodies and imagined the dreams locked up inside, but I also found elderly men poignant. Writing first-person short stories, for example, I made myself first an aging waiter, then an elderly subway guard. I'm sure that pretending to be a male observer was a way of avoiding my vulnerability as a female participant, but I was also trying to understand the perspective of age. I sensed that I would be profligate with time until I admitted it had an end—not just for other people, but for me, too.

Nonetheless, in my heart, I didn't believe it for a minute. Life stretched before me without end. I lived in the future. I wasted time.

Change seems recognizable only after it's happened, like putting one's foot down for a familiar stair—and it's not there. This was my state of mind in "Doing Sixty." I was off-balance but, as you'll see, also free and on a level at last. The stair of the "feminine" role was gone. So was the idea that I had to be chosen instead of making choices. It had taken a lot of living, plus time to metabolize that living, plus seeking out role models of great old women, plus realizing that my body knew how to age even if I didn't, to realize that the "endless" central years of life were over. A whole new and unimagined country lay beyond.

I don't know if the inspector and the novelist could have learned their wisdom earlier. Re-reading, I note that he said, "If I had my life over…." But for me, it was only *after* I'd become an old lady myself that I lost the habit of imposing my sentimental interpretation on old people. Only *after* I knew I needn't have children myself could I see them as short people and potential friends. Only *after* I'd connected with both ends of the spectrum did I understand why, as Native American and other ancient cultures tell us, the very young and the very old have more in common with each other than with people in the central years. Both are closer to the mystery.

I also realized that kids can't devote energy to the past, and elders can't project themselves into the future, so both have more ability to teach us how to live in the present. If you're in the youthful or central years of life when an obsession with the future is addictive, and your culture is telling you that future happiness is mysteriously dependent on buying things, you could benefit from hanging out with the very young or very old; yogis who are hiding in plain sight.

I would say that in my prolonged adulthood that stretched from ten years old to fifty and more, I'd devoted a whopping 60 percent of my brain cells to the future. By the time of "Doing Sixty," I was still devoting 20 percent to future imaginings, plus 20 percent to obsessing about my mistakes in the recent past, but 60 percent of my brain cells had become available to the present; maybe 80 on a good day when I felt a rush of pleasure in the ordinary, that sudden sense of well-being by which we know we are truly alive.

With another decade of perspective, I see that long years of ignoring the calendar and living outside the generational loop may have finally found a deeper use. They weren't so realistic at the time, but combined with a new sense of mortality for balance, they yield some valuable lessons. All come under the general heading: *Time is relative:*

❖ Working as a freelance writer plunged me into ever-new subjects, and then spending thirty-plus years as an itinerant feminist organizer took me into ever-new places. Both probably helped delude me into a feeling of timelessness. As you may have noticed when taking a new journey, the way there seems very long, yet coming home by the same route seems much shorter. That's because newness stretches out our experience of time, but familiarity shortens it. From this, I've learned a kind of intimate version of Einstein's Theory: If time is relative, doing new things actually makes us feel we've lived a longer life.

❖ I used to think that generations had to do only with age. Parents were always parents, children were always their children even after they grew up, and that was that. But over the years of the women's movement, I've noticed that daughters who grew up with feminism in the air and water are often older than their own mothers who did not. Because the daughters were encouraged to use their own will, find their own talents, they are grown-up in a way that wasn't encouraged in an earlier generation. Even when their mothers find their talents later in life, go back to college, or otherwise blossom into a life once denied them, the daughters are immensely proud of their mothers, *but as if they were their children.*

When I shared this insight with a young man who was the same age as those feminist daughters, he added another turn of the screw. Sons of mothers' who were encouraged to give birth to someone else, before giving birth to themselves, were treated, as he put it, "like the man of the family, like your mother's protector, even when you still wanted protection yourself." For mothers who had been raised to believe that maleness was everything, that a son would fulfill their own dreams of success in the world, this could force a son to behave as his mother's age peer, or husband and protector, or even father.

In other words, generations are relative, too.

❖ The valuing and naming of time is also relative, thus we speak of a passage like menopause in terms of loss. I, glad too that I've lived to see open discussion of this totally female event. Indeed, there is even a Broadway play called "Menopause: The Musical." But menopause is still medicalized as a problem to be remedied, and treated socially as an absence.

In fact, what women lose in those menopausal years is everything we needed to support another person. What we keep is everything we need to support ourselves.

❖ My inability to plan had little to do with living in a hazy future, and more to do with a lack of power and control. By my forties, I'd realized that planning ahead was one of the most reliable measures of class. Rich people plan for several generations forward; poor people plan for Saturday night. By that measure, even women born into powerful families are often lower class. They give control of their lives over to husbands, children, community, society.

In those years, I thought the sole answer was for women to take more control of our futures, and for men—especially powerful men—to learn the flexibility and spontaneity that women in general and the poor in particular have over-developed into an art form. Both are still goals; everything is about balance. But I realize now that the art of living in the present is not so much controlling time, it's losing track of time.

This is most likely to happen when we surrender to something we love to do: not because it's a demand, or an emergency, or an inability to do anything else. Seeking out what we love so much that we lose track of time when we're doing it—that goes beyond Einstein's theory and puts us into his life. He loved his work so much that he had to be careful while shaving; otherwise, he cut himself when a spontaneous idea struck.

That is a hint of the timeless Now.

Perhaps some of you are saying: No one can comprehend the end of our own consciousness; it's like trying to wrap our minds around infinity. That's true, yet flashes of boundarylessness, of merging with an idea, nature, the universe, all come pretty close. I've mostly depended on accidental life experiences to reveal them, but I know others who feel these mergings while looking into a tree or the ocean, practicing meditation, or living in such a meditative way that the act of drinking a glass of water or making a bed becomes a meditation in itself, with a focus on breath and body and moment. However they arrive, those selfless moments have been reported over millennia as joyful. As the mystics say, the secret of losing one's fear of death is to "die before you die;" that is, to experience egoless moments by staying open to them.

Perhaps some of you are wondering why I didn't learn this much earlier from meditation or any of the techniques that teach us to observe our thoughts, thus discovering an always-present-in-the-present observer. I think you're right. Those classic teachings may be the only way to be fully alive at any age. All I can say is that I was too Midwestern, too hooked on activism for that. But I do notice that friends who meditate regularly—which doesn't mean *not* thinking, as in the popular image designed make it seem impossible, but *observing* thinking—are more likely to feel linked to the universal. Meditation remains an intention in my brain cells devoted to the future.

Now, I owe a precious sense of mortality and time, and also a reminder of the unpredictability of everything, including my own decisions, to David, the friend I married six years after "Doing Sixty." Nothing could have been less expected or intended by either one of us, who were living quite happily on our own. Nothing could have been more incautious, short of jumping out of a plane without a parachute. He was a man living so much in the present that he wandered the world with few possessions, and would stop his car on the most dangerous freeway to rescue a wounded animal, or to set aside the body of a lifeless one with a few words of respect. A big gruff bear of a man, he would nonetheless pause on the beach to pick a tiny ladybug off the sand, and put it back on a leaf.

Because he lived in his heart even more than his head, he helped me to get there, too. Though he was younger than I, he died of an unexpected illness only a little more than three years later. Despite the shortness, despite the suffering of watching him suffer, I would not have missed or changed a thing. We both planted and grew in years that are supposed to be only those of harvest. He pushed and nudged and inspired and loved me out of old ruts and patterns and choices.

The bias of the air we breathe is that youth is exciting and age is sad. Not true. Our limited view of nature is that the harvest of life depends on the planting and growing that has gone before. Not true. We live in bodies full of cells that are constantly multiplying even as others are falling away. Each moment is a microcosm of past, present and future. There is no linear progression of time; there is no closure, just a connection that continues in a different way.

Whether we are eighty or eight, everything is present in the Now.

Doing Sixty

Doing Sixty

I belong to a generation of women who have never existed. Never in history . . . women who are outside of family, and whom society would like to silence.... It is a time for raising your head and looking at the view from the top of the hill, a view of the whole scene never before perceived.

Barbara Macdonald (1913 - 2000)[1]

Age is supposed to create more serenity, calm and detachment from the world, right? Well, I'm finding just the reverse. The older I get, the more intensely I feel about the world around me; the more connected I feel to nature, though I used to prefer human invention; the more poignancy I find not only in very old people, but also in children; the more likely I am to feel rage when people are rendered invisible, and also to claim my own place; the more I can risk saying "no" even if "yes" means approval; and most of all, the more able I am to use my own voice, to know what I feel and say what I think. In short, I can finally *express* without also having to *persuade.*

Some of this journey is uniquely mine and I find excitement in its solitary, edge-of-the-world sensation of entering new territory with the wind whistling past my ears. Who would have imagined, that I, once among the most externalized of people, would now think of meditation as a tool of revolution (without self-authority, how can we keep standing up to external authority)? or consider inner space more important to explore than outer space? or dismay even some feminists by saying that our barriers are also internal? or voice thoughts as contrary as: The only lasting arms control is how we raise our children?

On the other hand, I know this stage is a common one. I'm exploring the other half of the circle—something that is especially hard in this either/or culture that tries to make us into one thing for life, and treats change as if it were a rejection of the past. Nonetheless, I see more and more people going on to a future that builds on the past yet is very different from it. I see many women who spent the central years of their lives in solitary creative work or nurturing husbands and children—and some men whose work or temperament turned them inward too—who are discovering the external world of activism, politics, and tangible causes with all the same excitement that I find in understanding less tangible ones. I see many men who spent most of their lives working for external rewards, often missing their own growth as well as their children's, who are now nurturing second families and their internal lives—and a few women who are following this pattern too, because they needed to do the unexpected before they could feel less than trapped by the expected.

I'm also finding a new perspective that comes from leaving the central plateau of life, and seeing more clearly the tyrannies of social expectation I've left behind. For women especially—and for men too, if they've been limited by stereotypes—we've traveled past the point when society cares very much about what we do. Most of our social value ended at fifty or so when our youth-related powers of sexuality, childbearing, and hard work came to an end—at least, by the standards of a culture that assigns such roles— and the few powerful positions reserved for the old and wise are rarely ours anyway. Though this neglect and invisibility may shock and grieve us greatly at first, and feel like "a period of free fall," to use Germaine Greer's phrase, it also creates a new freedom to be ourselves—without explanation. As Greer concludes in *The Change,* her book about women and aging: "The climacteric marks the end of apologizing. The chrysalis of conditioning has once and for all to break and the female woman finally to emerge."[2]

From this new vantage point, I see that my notion of age bringing detachment was probably just one more bias designed to move older groups out of the way. It's even more self-defeating than most biases—and on a much grander scale—for sooner or later, this one will catch up with all of us. We've allowed a youth-centered culture to leave us so estranged from our future selves that, when asked about the years beyond fifty, sixty, or seventy—all part of the human life span if we escape hunger, violence, and other epidemics—many people can see only a blank screen, or one on which they project disease and dependency. This incomplete social map makes the last third of life an unknown country. It leaves men stranded after their work lives are over, but ends so much earlier for women that only a wave of noisy feminists has made us aware of its limits by going public with experiences that were once beyond its edge, from what Margaret Mead called "postmenopausal zest," to the news that raised life expectancies and lowered birth rates are making older people, especially older women, a bigger share of many nations, from Europe to Japan, than ever before in history. I hope to live to the year 2030, and see what this country will be like when one in four women is sixty-five or over—as is one in five of the whole population. Perhaps we will be become hardy perennials who "re-pot" ourselves and bloom in many times.[3]

More and more, I'm beginning to see that life after fifty or sixty is itself another country, as different as adolescence is from childhood, or as adulthood is from adolescence—and just as adventurous. At least it would be, if it weren't also a place of poverty for many, especially women over sixty-five, and of disregard for even more. If it's to become a place of dignity and power, it will require a movement as big as any other—something pioneers have been telling us for a long time. In 1970 when Maggie Kuhn was sixty-four, she founded the Gray Panthers, and also understood that young people were more likely to be allies of the very old than were the middle-aged, who assume a right to decide for both their children and their parents. Activist and writer Barbara Macdonald used her view as a lesbian living off the patriarchal map to warn us that feminism had failed to recognize women beyond family age as a center of activism and feminist theory.[4] Generations of what Alice Walker called "the Big Mama tradition" in the black community have provided us with role models of energized, effective, political older women. A few pioneering studies have told us to confront fears of aging and look at a new stage of life. For instance, Carnegie Corporation's Aging Society Project, predicted twenty years ago: "The increase of about thirty-five years in life expectancy in the 20th century is so large that we have almost become a different species."[5]

We may not yet have maps for this new country, but other movements can give us a compass. Progress seems to have similar stages: first, rising up from invisibility by declaring the existence of a group with shared experiences; then taking the power to name and define the group; then a long process of "coming out" by individuals who identify with it; then inventing new words to describe previously unnamed experiences (for instance, "ageism" itself); then bringing this new view from the margins into the center by means ranging from new laws to building a political power base that's like an internal nation; and finally maintaining a movement as stronghold of hope for what a future and inclusive world could look like—as well as a collective source of self-esteem, shared knowledge, and support.

Think about the pressure to "pass" by lying about one's age, for instance; that familiar temptation to falsify a condition of one's birth or identity and pretend to be part of a more favored group. Fair-skinned blacks invented "passing" as a term, Jews escaping anti-Semitism perfected the art, and the sexual closet continues the punishment. Pretending to be a younger age is probably the most encouraged form of "passing," with the least organized support for "coming out" as one's true generational self. I fell for this undermining temptation in my pre-feminist thirties, after I had made myself younger to get a job and write an exposé of what was then presented as the glamorous job of Playboy bunny—and was in reality an underpaid waitressing job in a torturing costume.[6] In the resulting confusion about my age, the man I was living with continued the fiction with all good will (he had been married to an actress who taught him that a woman was crazy to tell her real age), as did some of my sister's children, who thought she and I were two years younger. I perpetuated this difference myself for a couple of miserable years. I learned that falsifying this one fact about my life made me feel phony, ridiculous, complicit, and, worst of all, undermined by my own hand. It all had to do with motive, of course, because lying to get the job and write the exposé had been the same kind of unashamed adventure I undertook as a teenager when I made myself much older to get work selling clothes after school or dancing in operettas. Falsifying oneself out of insecurity and a need to conform is very different from defeating society's age bias. It's letting the age bias defeat you.

That was why, when I turned forty, I did so publicly—with enormous relief. When a reporter kindly said I didn't look forty (a well-meaning comment but ageist when you think about it), I said the first thing that came into my head: "This is what forty looks like. We've been lying so long, who would know?" That one remark got so many relieved responses from women that I began to sense the depth and dimension of age oppression, and how strong the double standard of aging remains. Since then, I've learned that for many women, passing and worrying about being found out is as constantly debilitating as an aching tooth—since one has to conceal the pain, perhaps more damaging.

I've met women who broke the law by forging their passports; who limited their lives by refusing to travel so they wouldn't have to get a passport; who told the men they married or lived with that they were as much as a decade younger; who had grown children whom they deceived; or who had mothers whose ages were not known until their deaths. I've listened to women who were working without health or pension plans because they feared having no jobs at all if their real ages were known; several who concealed academic degrees because their dates would put them over a mandatory retirement age; and one amazing seventy-three-year-old who had successfully convinced her employer that she was fifty and needed to be paid as a consultant rather than on the payroll—"for tax reasons." I remember the news story of a nameless woman in Israel who convinced her doctor that she was forty-eight in order to become eligible for the implantation in her womb of a fertilized egg, and so gave birth—at sixty. Her doctor said he never would have provided this service if he had known her real age. Meanwhile, France has just passed a law against "medically assisted procreation" for post-menopausal women—on the grounds that this possibility might cause women to further delay having children, and the government is already concerned about France's falling birthrate. It makes you understand why women lie.

If all the women now pressured to lie were to tell their ages, our ideas of what fifty-five or sixty or seventy-five looks like would change overnight. Even doctors might learn a thing or two. More important, women telling the truth without fear would be a joyous "coming out." Yet, as with lesbian women and gay men who have given the culture this paradigm of honesty, only people who freely choose to "come out" can diminish the fear that others feel.

Those are only the beginning of the parallels with other social justice movements. There is also the political impotence that comes from being invisible as a constituency and denying our generational peers. We lose their power and comfort, they lose our added talents and everyone is diminished. Conversely, once we identify, we both get and give strength. After a long conference on women and aging in Boston, I asked participants what in its program had been useful. More helpful than all the information, they said, was the act of walking past a sign in the hotel lobby that clearly announced a meeting of women over fifty. "For the first time since I was thirty-five," said one woman, "I felt proud of my age. I saw all those other terrific women walking in—as if it were the most natural thing in the world." Which, of course, it was.

On the other hand, segregation by age is just as unfair as that by race, sex, or anything else. We may decide to be with age peers, but it has to be free choice. The ability to do the job, pay for the apartment, or pass the entrance exam is the point—and it's no one's business why or how. Yet feminist groups, too, judge women by age instead of individuality. Right now, they are more concerned about attracting the young than including the old—to put it mildly. I myself have written many feminist statements that touch on different constituencies in order to be inclusive, but in retrospect, I think almost every racial, ethnic, or occupational group has got more mentions than women over, say, sixty-five. Moreover, in nearly twenty-five years of press conferences about the women's movement and questions from reporters,

I can't now think of one that focused on women over sixty.

The results of feeling alone, isolated, and no longer viable in society's eyes stretch from the largest and most obviously political to the deepest and most supposedly personal. As Barbara Macdonald has pointed out, major parts of our conversation at any age are about our bodies. Adolescent girls compare notes about breast development and menstrual periods, young women talk about contraception and pregnancy, and all of us run on about sexuality and general health. Yet older women are made to feel that their version of such discussions is somehow embarrassing, not worthy of younger listeners, or proof that older people talk constantly about aches and pains—though personally, I know of no evidence that an older woman who breaks her hip talks about it more than a young woman with a leg in a cast from a ski accident or a middle-aged man with a tennis elbow. Until a feminist generation began to talk about menopause and life after fifty, neither was an open topic of conversation; yet the interest must have been there. It has made a perennial best-seller of *Ourselves, Growing Older,* by the Boston Women's Health Book Collective, and also best-sellers of books by Germaine Greer, Gail Sheehy, and Betty Friedan.

It's in everyone's interest that women past fifty or sixty or even ninety continue health and body discussions. Not only do the women in question gain a community no one should be without, but they help younger women to fill in the blank screen of imagined futures.

The resistance to this movement is familiar too. Older employees are stereotyped as out of touch or less able to work, though the former is an individual question at any age and statistics on the latter show that, to the contrary, older employees are less likely to be absentee and more likely to be responsible. The usual tactic of divide and conquer is going full steam too, with younger people being told that older ones who resist retirement are taking their jobs away, just as women of every race were said to be taking away the jobs of men of color, or immigrants were said to be causing unemployment among the native born. Looking at each situation shows the facts to be quite different. With age especially, this tactic is usually employed by companies trying to fire experienced employees who earn more, and replace them with younger employees who earn less.

In recent years, I've noticed that even my accidental statement—"This is what forty looks like. We've been lying so long, who would know?"—is quoted without its second sentence. Instead of the plural that said we're all fine as we are—which was the point—only the singular was left, as if there were only one way to look. Small as this may be, it's a symbol of the will to divide and individualize. So is a telephone call I just got from *Redbook*. For an article on aging, the reporter was asking, "How do you stay young?"

There is no such thing as being individually free in the face of a collective bias. Just as with racism, anti-Semitism, or prejudice against all but the able-bodied, one is aware of fighting and escaping, even with success. Instead of treating my age as just another attribute, I found myself announcing it in any speech or public setting, whether age was relevant or not. It is one of the many ways we honor restrictions by striving to do their opposite.

In the past, I also put energy into trying to live up to society's expectations *and* resisting them. From my teenage years into my mid-thirties, the goal was to conform (or at least to rebel secretly). I felt an uncertainty, a lack of self-authority that came from a big dose of the "feminine" role, textbooks from which the female half of the human race was almost totally missing, and a fear of meeting my mother's fate of being poor, depressed, and alone with a child if I did not choose a conventional life. (Having not yet sorted out myth from reality, I didn't realize her fate *was* conventional.) After feminism arrived in my thirties to show me that women had a right to every human choice, I began conscious and open resistance. I found such usefulness and pleasure, such relief and companionship, in taking a different path openly that I assumed I was becoming as radical and rebellious as I could get.

Not only were other feminists and I treated as crazies—which we were, in the sense of wanting something that had never been—but unlike most feminists and women in general, I had skipped the years of raising a family and created a chosen family of friends, lovers, and colleagues instead. Furthermore, I'd begun to work full time in this longest of all revolutions. I felt lucky to be spending my days on what I cared about most, work so infinitely interesting, worthwhile, and close to the bone of my own and other women's hopes that it rarely seemed like work at all. Because I was traveling around the country as an organizer and as part of a speaking team, I was seeing women flower and change in a miraculous way that continues on a far larger scale now. Then, it was still a surprise every day, from the first sanity-saving realization "I am not alone" to the talent-freeing discovery "I am unique." Whether I was with Dorothy Pitman Hughes, a pioneer in community child care, or lawyer and feminist activist Florynce Kennedy, or organizer and writer Margaret Sloan, the most important thing we did was to make a space for women to come together—in groups that might be anything from a few dozen in a church basement to a few thousand in a lecture hall—and hear their experiences confirmed by each other's lives. That our team was composed of a black woman and a white woman together made audiences more diverse than either of us could have attracted alone and seemed to spread an implicit faith in crossing boundaries. In discussions that lasted longer than our speeches, women answered one another's questions. Men in the audience heard women telling the truth.

What I remember most about those years was being flooded with the frequent feeling: *If I'd done only this in my life and nothing more, it would have been enough.* Each day, I thought the next couldn't possibly be more intense and satisfying—and then it was.

After the first year or so of organizing had proved this changing consciousness was a rational contagion, *Ms.* magazine became one of the many new women-controlled entities to be born from the energy. Though I had stoutly maintained I was entering into this group effort for only two years, and then going back to my life as a freelance writer, working on *Ms.* magazine, helping to start other feminist groups, and traveling as an organizer became my life.

After almost two decades of no week without traveling, speaking, fund-raising, brainstorming, dead-lining, begging, arguing, and the incredible intensity of hope that any good movement is built on, I couldn't imagine that any future could be more rebellious or satisfying or stretched further from the rules. But I was also fragmented and burned out. I realized at the margins of my consciousness that the world was fading from color to shades of gray. Though not downtrodden, I felt down*pressed*—by pressures I myself had chosen. Even my cast-iron constitution was beginning to give way, and I felt more sharply than ever the unfairness of the pinched resources on which at *Ms.* and other parts of the movement were required to perform daily miracles, while testosterone-fueled corporations lavished millions on, say, one magazine prototype that failed, or a corporate takeover that lost jobs. Of course, there was always the joy of working with the people and possibilities I loved, but the very intensity of my feelings made me more conscious of what they deserved—and weren't receiving.

Nevertheless, as many women do, I went right on responding, explaining, responding again, reexplaining, and re-reexplaining as required, even if I was sometimes doing it on automatic pilot.

At the same time—perhaps because I was so drained, something in my unconscious knew I needed to look at this—I began thinking about the need to link self-esteem to revolution. In almost two decades of traveling, plus the years of reading letters to *Ms.* of such intensity and diversity that the Schlesinger Library cataloged them as a populist record of the movement,[7] I'd come to know the stories of brave and talented women of all classes, ages, races, sexualities, and abilities, too many of whom assumed they were somehow "not good enough," even though they were performing miraculous feats under hard circumstances. I'd read and heard too many valuable sentences prefaced with phrases like: "It's probably only me, but . . . ," suitable words, I sometimes thought, for almost any woman's epitaph. Sure enough, when I finally had a little quiet in which to think and write (thanks to the fact that two Australian feminists had come along with investment money to keep *Ms.* going when our shoestring had worn to a thread), I discovered I'd been responding to outside emergencies for so long that I'd lost what little I had of the muscle that allows us to *act* instead of *react*.

Though I'd been countering my childhood and "feminine" conditioning with an activism that was half the battle—it still was only half. I didn't regret one second of the years spent chipping away at a sexual caste system that oppresses women's spirits and distorts men's too, but I'd been submerging myself, not in the traditional needs of husband and children, true, but in the needs of others nonetheless. Having been bred by class and gender to know what other people wanted and needed better than I knew what I did, I had turned all my antennae outward. Focusing on women as a group had been a giant leap forward, for their needs were mine too. But no one could know my unique talents and demons unless I expressed them.

It wasn't a question of getting back into a balance between the internal and the external, the self and others. As a well-socialized woman, I'd never been in balance. I wouldn't have known balance if I'd tripped over it. Even thinking about it was a new event.

For three years, *Revolution from Within*,[8] the book that resulted from this exploring that began a few years after I turned fifty, was a living, breathing presence in my life. It helped me know with certainty that our inner selves are no more important than outer realities—but no less important either.

Could I have learned this earlier? I don't know. Certainly, I would have been a more effective activist if I had. I would have been better able to stand up to conflict and criticism, to focus on what I could uniquely do instead of trying to do everything, and to waste less time confusing motion with action. But perhaps I couldn't explore internally until I stopped living in an external pressure cooker. Or perhaps I had to exhaust myself on half the circle before I could appreciate the other half. In a larger sense, it doesn't matter. The art of life isn't controlling what happens—which is impossible—it's using what happens.

Gradually, I discovered I was researching and writing what I needed to learn. What I started out to address in other women, I myself shared: the need to treat ourselves as well as we treat others. It's women's version of the Golden Rule.

In fact, I have yet to meet a woman who has completely kicked the habit of leading a derived life that depends more on her sense of others than her sense of herself. Even if we've refused to be hyper-responsible for the welfare of a family, we often feel too responsible for what goes on at work. Even if we're no longer trying to surgically transplant our ego into the body of a husband or children, we still may be overly dependent on being needed—by coworkers and bosses, lovers and friends, even by the very movements that were intended to free us from all that.

For me, learning this lesson was definitely a function of age. I wasn't ready to admit how deeply into my brain cells and viscera the social role had permeated while I was still within the age range of its grasp.

Once I began to listen to my own authentic voice—or at least to realize I had one—I discovered a new answer to my earlier rhetorical question: How much more rebellious could

I get? The answer was: A lot. I found anger as a source of energy within myself. As in the wonderful phrase of Patricia Williams—writer, law professor, and African-American feminist—I found "a gift of intelligent rage."[9]

As it turns out, love and anger are both emotions of the free will, yet only love is acceptable for the powerless to express. For women or any category of people whose fair treatment would upset the social order, anger becomes the most punished emotion. Therefore, to show it is also a sign of freedom. It's an honesty without which love, too, eventually becomes a sham.

So for me, it was and is a step forward to say: I feel anger when I remember how much time I had to spend explaining myself, explaining what was wrong, explaining "what women want", or explaining at all. I feel anger that I had to fight against living in a culturally deprived, white-only box of the sort this society creates to limit our friends and keep our labels clear. I feel anger that I've studied history, watched television, and obeyed governments in which I saw so little that looked like my half of the human race or the diversity of the country. I feel anger that all of the above is still happening in varying degrees of painfulness; for instance, that I and others still require adjectives, while those who define go unadorned. Just what is the difference between a *woman* writer and a writer? a *black* surgeon and a surgeon? a *lesbian* athlete and an athlete? a *disabled* mathematician and a mathematician? Why does the operative definition of a special issue turn out to be any issue not important to the speaker? And why is the word "qualified" applied only to those who have to be more so? Why are women raped far away (say, Bosnia) called *victims,* while those raped nearby (say, a local campus) are playing *victim politics*?

Finally, I feel angry that the righteous anger I did manage to express in the past was denigrated as unprofessional or self-defeating, or more subtly suppressed when others praised me as calm, reasonable, not one of those "angry feminists." (How do we fall victim to the "good girl" syndrome? Let me count the ways.)

But it's a healthy anger that warms my heart, loosens my tongue, leaves me feeling more impatient and energized, and gives me a what-the-hell kind of courage. At last, I'm beginning to ignore the rules altogether—by just *not paying tribute to them,* whether by conforming *or* confronting. Now, messages I once heard only with my head go straight to my heart.

For instance, these words from a woman whose birth year I share, the late and well-loved poet Audre Lorde:

> I speak without concern for the accusations
> that I am too much or too little woman
> that I am too Black or too white
> or too much myself.[10]

Or these from writer and scholar Carolyn Heilbrun, about the heroine of the mysteries she wrote as "Amanda Cross"— who was therefore also Carolyn:

... she has become braver as she has aged, less interested in the opinions of those she does not cherish, and has come to realize that she has little to lose, little any longer to risk, that age above all, both for those with children and those without them, is the time when there is very little "they" can do for you, very little reason to fear, or hide, or not attempt brave and important things.[11]

In other words, I'm becoming more radical with age. I don't know why I'm surprised by this. When I was forty-five, I wrote an essay describing the female journey as the reverse of the traditional male one.[12] Men tend to rebel when young and become more conservative with age, but women tend to be more conservative when young and become rebellious as we grow older. I'd noticed this pattern in the suffragist/ abolitionist era, when women over fifty, sixty, even seventy were a disproportionate number of the activists and leaders— think of Sojourner Truth and Susan B. Anthony, or Elizabeth Cady Stanton and Ida B. Wells—but I'd assumed it was due to the restrictions placed on younger women by uncontrolled childbirth and their status as household chattel: hard facts that limited all but a few single or widowed white women, and all but even fewer free women of color. Yet when I looked at the current wave of feminism, I was surprised to find that the ages of activism weren't all that different. The critical mass were still women of thirty, forty, fifty or beyond—only a decade or so younger than their suffragist counterparts. I realized that most women in their teens and twenties hadn't yet experienced one or more of the great radicalizing events of a woman's life: marrying and discovering it isn't yet an equal (or even nonviolent) institution; getting into the paid labor force and experiencing its limits, from the corporate "glass ceiling" to the "sticky floor" of the pink-collar ghetto; having children and finding out who takes care of them and who doesn't; and, finally, aging, still the most impoverishing and disempowering event for women of every race and so the most radicalizing. To put it another way, if young women have a problem, it's only that they think there's no problem.*

I wrote that essay because I was angry with the media—though you probably would have had to be on LSD to sense it from the calm of my prose—for assuming that the male cultural pattern of rebelling in youth and then growing more conservative with age was the only one. Indeed, reporters still look for the red-hot center of feminist activism on campus—or in the male style of dropping out of the system, though it's more radical for women to drop in—thus missing the activist centers of battered women's shelters, rape crisis hot lines,

---

*Which makes the many organizations of young women active on their own behalf more remarkable. Their number is growing. For instance, the Third Wave (511 West 25th Street, New York, N.Y. 10001), a multiracial, direct-action group, whose first activity was Freedom Summer, 1992, a bus caravan that crisscrossed the country to register voters in poor areas; and Choice USA, a youth-led organization that trains local and national leadership (1010 Wisconsin Avenue, N.W., Suite 410, Washington, D.C. 20007), www.choiceusa.org. Go to femininist.com and feminist.org for links. There are many more such groups at a local level.

child support and custody actions, economic development groups, pink-collar organizing, and many other sources of energy. If my essay had little impact on journalists, however, I have to admit that it also had little impact on my own life. I still thought I was reporting on others, and failed to realize that this cultural pattern of growing more radical with age was also happening to me.

I don't know what I imagined the last thirty or forty years of my life were going to be. Perhaps just more of the same, for I thought that I had already disobeyed the rules. After all, I'd left my childbearing years behind without following the traditional pattern for women. Furthermore, I was constantly aware that very few people, male or female, could work full-time at what they loved without starving and thus I was a lucky exception. Or perhaps I'd just been confronted so often in my life with people who insisted, "You're so different from those other _____" (fill in the blank with the group of your choice), that I'd fallen into thinking I was an exception to the trends I myself observed.

What I'd forgotten is that patriarchy creates mega-patterns that affect us all—even if we forge different individual choices within them—just as do the mega-patterns of nationalism or racism. This amnesia on my part was all the more remarkable because I'd shared many of the experiences leading up to that more-rebellious-with-age conclusion. For instance:

❖ I, too, believed when I was in high school and college, as my textbooks led me to, that everything had been solved decades earlier by worthy but boring, asexual suffragists about whom I knew very little, except that I didn't want to be like them. *Today's young women are encouraged to feel somewhat the same way about feminists who preceded them, a conscious or unconscious way of stopping change by distorting the image of changemakers.*

❖ I,too, thought marriage would shape my life more than any other single influence—which was why I kept putting off the choice that seemed to put an end to all other choices. *Young women now can be more honest about delaying marriage or choosing a different path or continuing to make their own choices after marriage. But if they do marry, they still end up with a life more shaped by marriage than their husband's life is likely to be.*

❖ I, too, identified with every underdog in the world before realizing that women are primordial underdogs. *Today, many still take injustice more seriously if it affects any group except women. Women ourselves may support other causes before having the self-respect to stand up for our own.*

There's a lesson here about who's encouraged to have

a sense of belonging and who isn't. Whether the category is as specialized as "physicians" or as generalized as "white males," members of a powerful group are raised to believe (however illogically) that whatever affects it will also affect them. On the other hand, members of less powerful groups are raised to believe (however illogically) that each individual can escape their group's fate. Thus, cohesion is encouraged on the one hand, and disunity is fostered on the other.

For example, I would have been delighted to think that I, too, could grow more radical and rebellious with age but the habit of exempting myself won out. With few role models of daring, take-no-shit older women in my history books or my family history as transmitted to me (though both held many in reality)—and with even the rebellious older women I had written about consigned to the category of "other" prescribed by my reporter's role—my own future remained a hazy screen.

Since "radical" is often turned into a word as negative as "aging," perhaps I should explain why, as a person who came of age in the conservative 1950s, I came to believe radicalism was a good thing. There were two experiences that shaped its positive meaning for me, one of them a decade before feminism and the other in the way it came into my life.

The fall after graduating from college, I went to India on a year's fellowship. (Remember my tactic of delaying marriage? Well, India was not only a place I'd always wanted to go, but an escape from a very kind and tempting man to whom I was engaged and knew I shouldn't marry.) To my surprise, I found that I felt more at home and involved in India than I ever had in other countries not my own. I stayed on for another year after the fellowship doing freelance writing. In that diverse country that welcomes foreigners with the same equanimity that allowed it to absorb foreign cultures for centuries and yet remain itself, the students at the women's college of the University of Delhi accepted me as one of two Westerners to live there. They taught me to wear saris and were generally more instructive about India than was the curriculum, which was still shaped by the colonial system and treated England as the center of the universe. In the same period, I was also befriended by a group of gentle activists and intellectuals known as the Radical Humanists. From listening to their energetic analyzing of world events, I learned that "radical" didn't have to mean violent, extremist, or crazy, as a reading of U.S. newspapers had led me to believe. It could mean exactly what the dictionary said: going to the root.

Though many Radical Humanists, women and men, had started out as members of the Communist Party of India when it was supporting the Indian Independence Movement, they had left once the Party did an about-face during World War II and supported the British Raj—an evidence of its allegiance to Soviet needs rather than Indian autonomy. Like many friends who were Gandhians, and who also were to show me new alternatives, these activists had progressed

beyond such Marxist tenets as "the end justifies the means."
Their experiences caused me to rethink my romance
with Marxism, which had started in college when Joseph
McCarthy's persecution of actual or imagined Communists
made them seem admirable by comparison. As the Radical
Humanists pointed out, the means we choose dictate
the ends we achieve—so much so that one might more
accurately say, "the means become the ends." M.N. Roy, one
of their founders, wrote that "the end justifies the means
… eventually brought about the moral degeneration of the
international communist movement."[13]

As Gandhi also explained, using natural imagery: "the
means may be likened to a seed, the end to a tree."[14]

I remember my first experience with activism that
consciously reflected a future goal in its present tactic. I'd
been traveling through South India on my own, having
passed beyond the friendly chain of Radical Humanists in
the north. As I made my way down the coast from Calcutta,
I discovered that a Westerner in a sari was no more strange
than someone from a distant part of India, and that my
English-with-a-little-Hindi was as useful (or useless) as
some of the other fourteen major languages of India. In
the women's car of third-class trains and in public hostels,
I found myself struggling to respond to the very un-British,
thoroughly Indian habit of asking personal questions. In
my case, this meant probing everything from why I wasn't
married to whether I knew how to have fewer children—by

methods the husbands of these women couldn't discover.

When I went inland by rickety bus to visit one of the ashrams started by Vinoba Bhave—a disciple of Gandhi who was asking village landowners to give part of their acreage to the poor—Bhave and most of his coworkers had already left; not on one of their usual pilgrimages to ask for land donations, but walking from village to village through Ramnad, a nearby rural area where caste riots had broken out. Government officials in faraway Delhi had responded by embargoing all news coming out of the area and closing it off in the hope that burnings and killings could be kept from spreading.

Nonetheless, Bhave's teams had walked in on their own. Instead of asking people to stay in their houses, they were holding village meetings. Instead of a chain of vengeance, they were offering Gandhian nonviolence. Instead of weapons, they were carrying only a cup and a comb, knowing that if villagers wanted peace, they would feed and house the peacemakers, thus becoming part of the process.

Their problem was that no woman was left in the ashram to join a last team of three. Men couldn't go into the women's quarters to invite women out to meetings, and if there was no woman at the meeting, other women were unlikely to come anyway. The question was: Would I go with them? Bhave's coworkers assured me I wouldn't seem any more odd than others from outside the area. They themselves were trusted only because of their work in creating land trusts for the poor. Besides, part of their mission was to show villagers that people outside this isolated area knew and cared what was happening to them.

For the next few days, we walked from one village to the next—sitting under trees for meetings in the cool of the early morning, walking during the heat of the day, and holding more meetings around kerosene lamps at night. Mostly, we just listened. There were so many stories of atrocities and vengeance, so much anger and fear that it was hard to imagine how it could get better. But gradually, people expressed relief at having been listened to, at seeing neighbors who had been too afraid to come out of their houses, and at hearing facts brought by Bhave's team. The rumors were even more terrible than the events themselves. To my amazement, long and emotion-filled meetings often ended with village leaders pledging to take no revenge on caste groups whose members had attacked in neighboring villages, and to continue meetings of their own.

Each morning, we set off again along paths shaded by palms and sheltered by banyan trees, cut across plowed fields, and waded into streams to cool off then let our homespun clothes dry on us as we walked. In the villages, families shared their food and sleeping mats with us, women taught me how to wash my sari and wash and oil my hair, and shopkeepers offered us rice cakes and sweet milky tea in the morning. I found there was a freedom in having no possessions but a sari, a cup, and a comb, and, even in the midst of turmoil, a peacefulness in focusing only on the moment at hand. I remember this as the first time in my life that I was living completely in the present.

Toward the end when the violence had quieted down, my unseasoned feet had become so blistered that infection set in. I hitched a ride in an oxcart back to the bus route to the ashram. Nevertheless, I ended those days with no regret. I had learned the truth of what I once disdained as an impractical and impossibly idealistic Gandhian saying: *If you do something the people care about, the people will take care of you.*

From our team leader, a no-nonsense man in his seventies who had devoted his life to this kind of direct action—and to Gandhian tactics that were a microcosm of their goal—I also remember this radical advice:

> *If you want people to listen to you, you have to listen to them.*
>
> *If you hope people will change how they live, you have to know how they live.*
>
> *If you want people to see you, you have to sit down with them eye-to-eye.*

Most of us have a few events that divide our lives into "before" and "after." This was one for me.

When I finally traveled back home to my own country,

these lessons didn't seem very portable. If "radical" is often misunderstood now, consider how it sounded in 1958, with Eisenhower still President and fears of McCarthyite persecution still in the air. At least at a visible level, there was no populist movement against the Cold War, no women's movement, not even an understanding yet that hunger existed in this country, and only a few groups working on such issues as fallout from nuclear testing and civil rights protests that were not yet a movement. As for India, it hadn't yet appeared on this nation's media radar as anything other than a place of former British power and present poverty. Even the Beatles hadn't discovered India yet. Indeed, there were no Beatles. If I brought up India as a country I'd just returned from, an island of polite silence would appear in the conversation—and then the talk of other things would flow right on around it.

I was in shock myself. I was seeing my own overdeveloped country through the eyes of the underdeveloped country for the first time. In search of imagery for this revelation, I remember saying to all who would listen, "Imagine a giant frosted cupcake in the midst of hungry millions." What really ran through my head like a naïve mantra was: *This can't last.*

Because India had accustomed me to seeing a rainbow of skin colors, I was also realizing belatedly that in my own multiracial country, you could go snowblind from white faces in any business area or "good" neighborhood. True, skin color in India often carried the cruelty of caste, but a South

Indian Brehmam might have darker skin than a North Indian harijan (the Gandhian term for "untouchable"), and since all had suffered collectively under British rule, there was at least a striving for a shared identity. Furthermore, Indians described nuances of color as unselfconsciously as any other aspect of appearance. It made me realize that the deafening silence about color in my own upbringing had not been polite, but just another way of saying that being anything other than white was too uncomfortable to be commented upon. I began to see how caste-divided this country was and how dishonest we were in discussing it. This training has been so effective in my case that I had to experience a different society in order to see it.

Sometimes my culture shock took surrealistic for *Ms.* In New York, where I had been sleeping on my friends' living room floors while trying to find a job, I remember insisting on riding in the front seat with taxi drivers. My sense memory of sitting in an Indian tonga—a two-wheeled cart pulled by a man riding a bicycle or running between the staves—was so strong that I couldn't handle being driven by another human being. Of course, a Calcutta tonga wallah had little to do with a New York taxi driver, but the images of the recent past were still imprinted on my eyes and I was viewing the world through them. I alternated between trying to explain what I'd experienced in India and leaving gatherings I couldn't handle because the contrast between them and what I was still seeing in my mind's eye.

In other words, I must have been a terrible pain in the ass.

The more I became acclimated to my own country, however, the more India began to seem like two years dropped out of my life—a time whose intensity I would never be able to match and whose lessons I could never make use of. Some of my trying to explain my experience was really trying to catch what was slipping away. Though I attempted to work in student politics this also didn't yet exist as a movement. I was far too broke and impatient to consider any graduate school.

Finally, I began to work as a freelance writer, but the assignments I could get as a "girl reporter" often widened the gap between what I was working on and what I cared about. I was drawn to the civil rights and anti-Vietnam movements that were becoming public events by then, but they were not the assignments available to female freelancers. I found myself paying the rent with humor and advice pieces for women's magazines (while going to a school desegregation rally in Virginia or a civil rights march in Washington); writing about the New York mayor's wife or a fashion designer because I was impressed to get a freelance assignment from The *New York Times* (while lobbying for Peace Corps volunteers to go to communities in India); profiling actors, dancers, and other celebrities for various magazines and newspapers (while organizing with writers and editors to refuse to pay that portion of our taxes that went to the Vietnam war); and writing about the "ins" and "outs" of pop culture for *Life* (while trying to get Cesar Chavez and his new United Farm Workers on the cover of *Time* as protection against threats on his life from California growers).

It wasn't that I disliked what I was doing. On the contrary, I liked Mary Lindsay, the mayor's wife, I loved writing satire for an *Esquire* campus issue or *That Was the Week That Was* on television, and I enjoyed learning about people and their work worlds while profiling them, from James Baldwin and Margot Fonteyn to Dorothy Parker and Truman Capote. But I never felt fully engaged, as if I were leading my own authentic life rather than one derived from others. Some of the tactics of those anti-Vietnam days made me feel more estranged than I had in India, where I had absorbed the idea that violent means are unlikely to reach a peaceful end— that ends and means are a seamless web. This philosophy wasn't always guiding the most public events of the peace movement.

When *New York* magazine was founded—aided in part by a group of us who were to be its regular writers—this gap between my work and my interests narrowed. At least I could write about electoral politics, social justice movements, and neighborhood organizing in New York; assignments that other magazines and newspapers usually gave to male reporters. But I was still a long way from the hands-on, organic, personal kind of activism I had glimpsed in India. Indeed, I had put it out of my mind.

In the movements of the 1960s, there was a saying: "You

only get radicalized on your own concerns." That was to prove true again in the way feminism arrived in my life.

It wasn't the first brave, reformist variety of the mid-1960s that woke me up. Though I was old enough to be part of the *Feminine Mystique* generation, I wasn't living in the suburbs, wondering why I wasn't using my college degree. I had ended up in the workforce many of these other women were then longing to enter. Though college had taken me out of my blue-collar Toledo neighborhood and made me a middle-class person, I shared the reaction of many working-class women and women of color to this early reformist feminism: *I support women who want to get out of the suburbs and into jobs,* I thought to myself, *but I'm already in the workforce and getting screwed. The women's movement isn't for me.* Given the contrast between India and this country's share of the world's resources, I also had another reservation: *Sure, women should get a fair share of the pie wherever we are, but what we really need is a new world pie.*

By the end of the 1960s, younger women were coming out of the civil rights and peace movements with similar feelings. They had a new phrase, "women's liberation," which addressed all women as a caste. Instead of integrating current systems, they were taking on patriarchy and racism at their base. Instead of trying to make "feminine" equal to "masculine," they were joining all human qualities into a full circle that was available to everyone.

At their speak-outs, I listened to stories of experiences

I, too, had known, but had never put into words. When I covered as a reporter an early feminist hearing on abortion, I heard personal testimonies to the sufferings brought on by having to enter a criminal underworld. I had had an abortion too, but I'd been lucky enough to be in England, where laws were slightly less punishing. It was just after college, but I never forgot the weeks of panic before I found a doctor, or how it changed my life to be able to continue the trip to India that was about to begin; yet I'd never spoken to anyone about this major experience in my life. Since one in three or four women had undergone an abortion even then, I began to wonder why it was illegal; why our reproductive lives were not under our own control; and why this fundamental issue hadn't been part of other social justice movements.

It was a time of epiphanies. I remember sitting amazed in front of my television set watching Anne Koedt, Anselma Dell'Olio, Betty Dodson, and other early feminists talk about sexuality on an obscure local show. It was the first time I'd ever heard women being sexually honest in public (it was rare enough in private) or taking on Freud's myth of the vaginal orgasm (about which Koedt had just written an essay that was to become a classic).[15] I started asking myself why women were supposed to have sex but not talk about it; why Freud got away with calling women "immature" for failing to have a male-fantasy orgasm; and why the so-called sexual liberation movement of the 1960s had been mostly about making more women sexually available on male terms.

God may be in the details, but the goddess is in the questions. Once we begin to ask them, there's no turning back. Instead of trying to fit women into existing middle-class professions or working-class theories, these radical feminist groups assumed that women's experience could be the root of theory. Whether at speak-outs or consciousness-raising groups, "talking circles" or public hearings, the essential idea was: *Tell your personal truth, listen to other women's stories, see what themes are shared, and discover that the personal is political.*

I'm not sure feminism should require an adjective. Believing in the full social, political, and economic quality of women, which is what the dictionary says "feminism" means, is enough to make a revolution in itself. But if I had to choose only one adjective, I still would opt for *radical* feminist. I know our adversaries keep equating that word with *violent* or *man-hating, crazy* or *extremist*—though being a plain vanilla feminist doesn't keep one safe from such epithets either. Neither does saying, "I'm not a feminist, but . . . ." Nonetheless, *radical* seems an honest indication of the fundamental change we have in mind: the false division of human nature into "feminine" and "masculine" is the root of all other divisions into subject and object, active and passive, and—the beginning of hierarchy. Since that division comes from the patriarchal need to control women's bodies as the means of reproduction—a control that racial "purity" and caste and class systems are built on—digging out the "masculine/feminine" paradigm undermines all birth-based hierarchies, and alters our view of human nature, the natural world, and the cosmos itself. Just a few little things like that.

Everything comes together once we've found the work for which we are suited. I've been traveling around this country every week for most of the past twenty-five years, working with many women and some men in the kind of direct-action organizing I first saw and was so magnetized by in India. But only recently have I understood the resonance between what I have been doing and that long-ago and long-buried turning point. I realize that the wisdom of our Ramnad team leader still holds true: *you have to listen. . . . you have to know . . . you have to sit down eye-to-eye.*

As for the Gandhian adage, *If you do something the people care about, the people will take care of you,* I have to admit there is a big difference here. Walking from village to village could get you arrested, and having to pay for your own airline ticket is very different from hitching a ride on a bullock cart. Still, like other traveling feminists or organizers for other movements who bring hope in a commonsense way, I do notice that the ticket clerk sometimes saves three seats across so I can sleep; the flight attendant slips me a healthier meal from first class; the airport cleaning woman stops to tell me about the latest woman candidate from her neighborhood; a woman now able to mother other women stocks our car with spring water and apples for our long drive to the next event; and even such brief contact as seeing a woman standing in a highway toll booth can yield good advice. "It's going to rain, honey," one said kindly to me last week. "Want to borrow my umbrella?"

A movement is only composed of people moving but to feel its warmth and motion around us is the end as well as the means.

Even our faults can be useful if we're willing to be honest about them. Because I was scared to death of public speaking, I often began lectures by explaining that only the women's movement had given me a reason worth making a damn fool of myself, that I'd never spoken publicly at all until I was in my mid-thirties, and that, if I could do it, anyone could. It was also this fear that led me to speaking with a partner in the beginning—which turned out to be a helpful tactic. It's this fear now that makes me look forward to a discussion time in which the audience takes over and creates its own organizing meeting. Invariably, the result is better than anything I or any single speaker could produce. In this way, I've learned that being able to use all of ourselves, whether positive or negative, is a good sign that we're doing the right thing.

I've also continued to learn from the collective wisdom of audiences, the late-night groups that gather after meetings, the people who stop me in the street to tell me stories of changes in their lives, people who write letters that should be books, populist researchers who send clippings with crucial passages marked, strangers who share what might be difficult to say to friends, and people in groups everywhere who are valuable advisers about what I or others could be doing better.

I've always been hooked on this "found wisdom," as I've come to think of it. When I went back to India almost twenty years after my student days, I discovered again that this form of populist teaching is a better aid to decision-making than most academic teaching. For example, I met with Indira Gandhi—then prime minister, though she had been a lonely and uncertain daughter of a Prime Minister when I first saw her—and she told me the story of her own third-class travels around India as a young mother in crowded women-only railway cars like the ones I remembered. On learning that she had only two children, women invariably asked her: "How did you do it?" And often: "How can I keep my husband from knowing? How can I keep him from thinking I'll be unfaithful?"

As prime minister, she defied population experts who insisted that poor and illiterate women didn't want birth control, or couldn't understand it until they became literate, or would accept it only if their husbands approved. She instituted family planning programs that were the first to offer women contraception in private. She also offered small financial rewards for men who agreed to be sterilized, and told health workers to explain to them that this way, husbands would know if their wives were being unfaithful.

Those measures were very controversial but more effective than the conventional ones. She received delegations of grateful women, and also criticism within her own country and in international circles for encouraging male sterilization. But the day we talked, she seemed unperturbed. She had never forgotten the words or the desperation of her populist women teachers.

On this same trip in the late 1970s, I was often told by academics and reporters in India's big cities that feminism was a Western phenomenon, that it had no roots in India. But unknown to many in the cities, a movement called Stree Shakti Jagritti (Women's Power Awakening) had been organizing conferences and padyataras (foot journeys) through rural India. Combining women's issues with the teachings of Gandhi and Vinoba Bhave, both of whom honored populist women teachers by saying that only awakening the inner strength of women could overcome India's obstacles, this movement had been working since the 1950s on everything from literacy campaigns to giving women small loans so they could produce and sell vegetables or handicrafts and wouldn't be forced into poverty and prostitution. At the very time I was being told that feminism was peculiar to the West, 10,000 members of this loose federation of women workers were marching from village to village, asking women about their problems, helping them to organize, offering the principles of self-strength and nonviolence—just as we had done in a much smaller way two decades before. Thanks to funds and women from the poor areas in which the work was being done, 75,000 women participated in the second padyatara.[16]

Now there is much more acknowledgment of the role of Indian feminist groups, urban as well as rural, in working against everything from sexual harassment in the workplace (often called Eve teasing in the Indian media) to the dowry murders that still take place when a husband or his family, wishing to acquire a second dowry, cause the "accidental" death of his first wife. The truth is that every country has its own organic feminism. Far more than communism, capitalism, or any other philosophy I can think of, it is a grassroots event. It grows in women's heads and hearts.

Though each day or week or month seems like a morass of happenstance and bewildering detail, one of the great advantages of age is a longer view that suddenly reveals patterns. An internal voice, an intrinsic set of values, a DNA that is powerful and unique within each of us—something has been organizing that morass of detail. For instance, it took me years to see the connections between discussions with Indian women in a third-class railroad car and the feelings that finally gave me the courage to speak in public, or between walking in Ramnad and getting on planes to unknown places with my speaking partners. I'm looking forward to the still longer views that reveal more patterns, for they tell us what is true within us. That means we know what should be continued.

I also see patterns of my resistance to what I knew in my heart I should do. Some people hang on to the familiar and the things they already know out of fear of the new. Others do it out of defiance of those who say we should change. The latter has always been my drug of choice. It's taken me a long time to realize that when I said so defiantly at fifty, "I'm going to go right on doing everything I did at thirty or forty," this was not progress. I was refusing to change and thus robbing myself of the future. I'm indebted to Robin Morgan for reminding me that for women like us, defiance for defiance's sake is a political version of a face-lift—a denial of change.

Probably, hanging on to the past brings more destruction than any other single cause. It's the strict constructionists who prefer a literal U.S. Constitution to the mechanisms for change that were the greatest creation of its framers. It's the Muslim fundamentalists who worship the past and ignore the reformist spirit with which Muhammad viewed the future, including the status of women. It's the backward-looking Christian literalists who interpret religious teachings in a way that consolidates their power. It's the fearful politicians who cite their version of the "good old days." Nostalgia may be the most tempting and deceptive form of opposition to change. In truth, no day or situation is identical to any other. To resist this constancy of change is to be as ridiculous as I was when I sat in front with a New York taxi driver. It's to be as dangerous as fundamentalists who bring glorification of death out of the past and into a nuclear present.

If clinging to the past is the problem, embracing change is the solution. If we remember that our tactics must always reflect our goals, there will be a flexible structure of continuing change—not to mention greater success. After all, there's no such thing as killing for peace, strengthening people by making their decisions for them, or suppressing dissent to gain the freedom to dissent.

There's also no such thing as being fully conscious in the present while preoccupied with the past *or* the future. When I was in my twenties and thirties, I had a habit of mind that I just accepted then, but realize now was robbing me of living the present. I used to fantasize pleasurably about being very old. Some part of my consciousness must have decided that only an acerbic, independent old lady would finally be free of the vulnerability and lack of seriousness that attach to female human beings while playing the "feminine" role is still an imperative. Only much later would I no longer be an interchangeable moving part, "a pretty girl," a group rather than an individual. Fortunately, by the time I was in my late thirties, feminism had helped me to understand that I could fight the role instead of wishing my life away. It makes no more sense to wish for age than to fear it. But not until I was past fifty did I read Carolyn Heilbrun's *Writing a Woman's Life* and understand that many women become ourselves after fifty, and thus my odd habit of mind had a good political reason.

What we all need, whatever our age, are personal role models of living in the present—and a change that never ends. We need to know that life past sixty or seventy or eighty is as much an adventure as it ever was, perhaps more so for women, since we are especially likely to find new territory once the long plateau of the "feminine" role is over. Explorers of this later-in-life region have always existed in some number, but now their lights dancing on the path ahead will guide many more.

I think of Frieda Zames, who at the age of sixty-two was answering reporters' questions about how she successfully integrated the Empire State Building as part of a class action suit against a number of hotels and office buildings that were not accessible to the disabled. In her fifties, her work also helped put lifts on New York buses so disabled passengers could ride and made New York polling places accessible to disabled voters for the first time. After retiring as a professor of mathematics, she had more time for Disabled in Action, the civil rights group with which she worked.[17] Felled early by polio, she spent her childhood in a hospital, and then became a mathematician—only to be told that high schools would not hire disabled teachers. She got an advanced degree, but discovered that being a woman was even more of a disability than getting around on crutches or a motorized scooter—at least, in the eyes of the all-male technological institute where she taught—so she became an activist twice over.

I think of Charlotta Spears Bass, who was a pioneering

newspaper reporter into her sixties. She then used her expertise on issues to begin another career. At the age of seventy, she became the Progressive Party's candidate for Congress from California. At seventy-two, she ran on that ticket against Richard Nixon—thus becoming the first black woman to run for the vice-presidency of the United States. I wish I had known her when I was struggling against being a "girl reporter" in the 1960s, for she had begun work as a journalist in 1900 at the age of twenty. She became the editor of a small newspaper and crusaded against the Ku Klux Klan and segregated housing, for women in political office and for early efforts to ban the atomic bomb. As a candidate, her slogan was "Win or lose, we win by raising the issues." She died in 1969 at the age of eighty-nine, knowing she had helped to put civil rights, women's rights, and peace on the national agenda.[18]

I think of Mary Parkman Peabody, a Boston Brahmin by birth and marriage. In 1964, at the age of seventy-two—without telling her son, who was then governor of Massachusetts—she left for a civil rights demonstration being held in Florida by Martin Luther King, Jr.. When she was jailed for sitting in at a segregated motel dining room, she made national headlines because of her illustrious family and her status as the widow of an Episcopal bishop. At a press conference, she commented cheerfully that the jail was very clean, there were beautiful flowers outside it, and she had enjoyed eating hominy grits with her fingers. Well into her eighties, she continued to demonstrate for civil rights, against the war in Vietnam, and against military spending. When she died at eighty-nine, obituaries called her "a prominent civil rights and antiwar activist," and only mentioned her illustrious family in passing. To this day, she is a symbol of rebellion for women born into a class trained not to rebel.[19]

I think of Edith Big Fire Johns, who began a new career at seventy-five. As a representative of Travelers and Immigrants Aid at Chicago's O'Hare Airport, she received babies arriving from Korea and Romania for adoption, helped African students and Asian immigrants coming to this country for the first time, and talked to runaways who felt they had no home but the airport. Having earned her nursing degree in 1937—one of the first Native American women to do so—she had a long career in the profession, and was one of the first staff members of the Native American Educational Services College, the only private Indian college in this county. At sixty-five, she joined the Peace Corps as a nurse on the island of Dominica, and traveled to meet with indigenous peoples in Australia and New Zealand. She returned home to teach the Indian beadwork at which she was expert as a member of both the Winnebago and Nez Percé tribes, and to help others in the Indian community to maintain tribal values in the midst of urban life. She did all that before starting an end-of-life career in which she could meet "People from parts unknown." She died in 1997 at eighty-three after two trips to Israel in her last two years, always seeking new understandings.

I think of Carrie Allen McCray, whose fresh and true poetry she only began to write seriously at seventy-three and who began publishing and giving poetry readings at eighty. The daughter of one of the first black lawyers and a mother who was a charter member of the National Association for the Advancement of Colored People in 1917, she herself was a social worker and professor of sociology in South Carolina and Alabama. With a memory that stretches from the Harlem Renaissance to the poetry of Sonia Sanchez and Sharon Olds, she began work on a novel about her mother, her grandmother who was a former slave, and her grandfather who was a Confederate general. Widowed by a husband whose work as a journalist she admired but who said, "I'm the writer in the family," she began to write every day. As she said, "I get up writing." Here are some of her words:

> Nobody wrote a poem
> about me
> In ugly tones they
> called me "Yaller Gal"
> How lovely to have been
> born black or brown
> Pure substance the artist
> could put his pen to
> Not something in between—
> diluted, undefined, unspecific
> I search the poets

for words of me
Faint mention in Langston Hughes'
Harlem Sweeties, I think,
yet I'm not sure
So full of "caramel treats,"
"brown sugars" and "plum
tinted blacks," it was
Soft, warm colors
making the poets sing
I, born out of history's
Cruel circumstance,
inspired no song
and nobody wrote a poem[20]

I think of Esther Peterson, born in 1906, a tall, slender young woman with brown braids encircling her head, who came out of Utah to become a labor organizer in the sweatshops of New England and the South. In the lonely years between suffrage and modern feminism, she carried the heart and conscience of the women's movement—learning from Eleanor Roosevelt to "draw a wider circle" around issues. In her fifties, she became head of the Women's Bureau under President Kennedy, a man she had educated on labor issues when he was a young Congressman. In the Johnson and Carter administrations, she was a voice for consumers, and at eighty-six she was appointed by President Clinton to represent the United States at the first United

Nations session of his administration. She knew the U.N. well, having pioneered its international listing of products considered dangerous in their country of manufacture but "dumped" in other countries, a listing opposed by many U.S. corporations and the Reagan administration. In her eighties, she founded the United Seniors' Health Cooperative to help older people become informed consumers of health care and health insurance.[21] She was always on the path ahead.

Now that I am finally retrieving the importance of India in my life, I think most of all of sitting on a New Delhi veranda in the 1970s, drinking tea with Kamaladevi Chattopadhyay, whose first name was (and is) enough to identify her in many countries of the world. Biographical dictionaries list her as "freedom fighter, social worker, writer." In the 1950s, when I first met her, she was in her fifties and already a legend for her leading role in the Freedom Struggle with Gandhi and Nehru—an activism for which she spent five years in British jails—and for her pioneering of the Indian handicraft movement. Our meeting was arranged by my oldest friend in India, Devaki Jain, because we both wanted to ask Kamaladevi's advice. Since Gandhi's nonviolent tactics were so well suited to women's movements around the world, we hoped to study his letters and writings, distill what was most useful, and create a kind of Gandhian/feminist handbook.

Kamaladevi listened to us patiently. Only at the end did she say, "Of course, Gandhi's tactics were suited to women—that's where he learned them." It was a sudden understanding that made us all laugh; one more instance of history lost. We had been attracted to what once was ours.

When I returned home, I lost track of Kamaladevi. I knew only that she had continued to travel the world into her eighties, helping other countries to preserve their creativity and culture in a handicraft industry, too. But I always remembered this woman who taught us women's history over a cup of tea, while continuing to make history herself.

She died at the age of eighty-five on her way to make a speech, effective to the last. Devaki Jain wrote a moving tribute to her: "I weep for her absence—a central support for realistic idealism. . . . She made museums appear like bread or water—things without which one could not live." Devaki described how Kamaladevi, asked to join dignitaries on a podium and light a lamp celebrating the golden jubilee of the All India Women's Conference, had said just a year before she died, "I have never gone on to a raised platform, it connotes hierarchy, distance." As Devaki explained, "She lit the lamp at the back of the hall, to the delight of the last rows.[22]

This is not to say that all of us have to do illustrious deeds, but quite the contrary, that all our deeds are illustrious. How we speak to each other, how our bodies feel, what we wear, how we work, what we buy, what we eat, whom we love—all these are part of the impact of our lives. Indeed, I'm not sure we have any idea which of our actions will be important while we are doing it.

To get us out of any sober, historic, or otherwise intimidating mood, I'll risk placing a poem here. Nothing is accomplished without making fools of ourselves and poetry for me is like singing in the shower. I also understood while writing it that groups of women mentioned here might have little choice as to how they had dressed or acted—but this poem refused to be politically correct. Even its title is only the answer that popped out when someone asked me what I planned for my old age: "I Hope To Be an Old Woman Who Dresses Very Inappropriately."

> *Women in business*
> *Dress in man-style suits*
> *And treat their secretaries*
> *In a man-style way.*
>
> *Women on campus*
> *Wear "masculine" thoughts*
> *And look to daddy for*
> *Good grades.*
>
> *Married women*
> *Give their bodies away*
> *And wear their husbands'*
> *Wishes.*
>
> *Religious women*
> *Cover sinful bodies*
> *And ask redemption from god*

Not knowing
She is within them.

That's why I'll always love
The fat woman who dares to wear
A red miniskirt
Because she loves her woman's body.
The smart woman who doesn't go to college
And keeps possession of her mind.
The lover who remains a mistress
Because she knows the price of marrying.
The witch who walks naked
And demands to be safe.
The crazy woman who dyes her hair purple
Because anyone who doesn't love purple
Is crazy.

Dear Goddess: I pray for the courage
To walk naked
At any age.
To wear red and purple,
To be unladylike,
Inappropriate,
Scandalous and
Incorrect
To the very end.

As you can see, I've come to realize the pleasures of being

a nothing-to-lose, take-no-shit older woman; of looking at what once seemed to be outer limits but turned out to be just road signs. For instance:

❖ I used to take pleasure in going to a feminist Seder every year, subverting that ancient ceremony by including women in it. In our Women's Haggadah, we honored not only Deborah, Ruth, and other heroines of the Bible, but also our own foremothers. "Why have our Mothers on this night been bitter?" we read together. "Because they did the preparation but not the ritual. They did the serving but not the conducting. They read of their fathers but not of their mothers."[23]

Lately, however, I've been wondering: Why start with anything that must be so changed, so fought *against?* Why not begin with the occasions of our own lives and create the ceremonies we need for births or marriages, adopting friends as chosen family or setting off on a new adventure, recognizing divorce as a life passage, or a new home as the symbol of a changing self? Having learned the pleasures of ritual, I'm thinking of founding a service: "Ceremonies to Go."

❖ I used to pass urban slums or rows of poor houses anywhere and compulsively imagine myself living there: *What would it be like?* It was a question of such fearsome childhood power that I only recently realized it had fallen away. It's simply gone. The deep groove worn by such imagining has finally been filled by years of words written and deeds done, crises survived and friends as family, work done with and for others and thus an interdependence that lets me relax. I no longer fear ending up where I began.

❖ I used to indulge in magical thinking when problems seemed insurmountable. Often, this focused on men, for they seemed to be the only ones with power to intercede with the gods. Now it has been so long since I fantasized a magical rescue that I can barely remember the intensity of that longing. Instead, I feel my own strength, take pleasure in the company of friends, male and female, who are mortals. I no longer believe in gods, except those in each of us.

❖ I used to think that continuing my past sex life was the height of radicalism. After all, women too old for childbearing were supposed to be too old for sex. Becoming a pioneer dirty old lady seemed a worthwhile goal—which it was, for a while. But continuing the past even out of defiance is very different from progressing. Now I think: Why not take advantage of the hormonal changes that age provides to clear our minds, sharpen our senses, and free whole areas of our brains? Even as I celebrate past pleasures, I wonder: Did I sometimes confuse sex with aerobics?

❖ I used to be one of the majority of Americans whose

greatest fear was dependency in old age—a fear that must have roots other than economic, for it is also prevalent among women and the racial groups of men least likely to be poor. Then I listened to the historian Gerda Lerner question this fear among a group of middle aged women gathered to talk about aging. As she pointed out, we don't fear dependency in the early years of life. On the contrary, we understand that being able to help dependent children find what they need can be a gift in itself. Why shouldn't we feel the same about the other end of life? Why shouldn't the equally natural needs of age be an opportunity for others to give? Why indeed? Now I wonder if women's fear of dependency doesn't stem from being too much depended upon. Perhaps if we equalize the giving of care—with men, with society—this will bring a new freedom to receive.

❖ I used to think that uprooting negative childhood patterns was a personal activity reserved for individuals. Now I wonder if this familiar healing process wouldn't benefit whole nations and races too. In the country in which I live, for example, there is a glorification of violence and a willful denial of how much it hurts—not to mention how much of this hurt is passed on to future generations. I wonder if we're collectively doomed to keep repeating violent patterns until we admit the hurt that took place in this nation's childhood: the reality of genocide that wiped out millions of indigenous peoples and all but destroyed hundreds of major cultures, plus the still only half-admitted realities of slavery and its legacy within each of us. I'm happy about the Holocaust Museum in Washington, D.C., for I know our government refused to admit thousands of Jews until it was too late, and, I am also glad that it is calling attention to current Holocausts. But we also need to have a Native American Museum which finally admits that the "uninhabited" Americas were home to as many people as Europe, and a Middle Passage Museum to memorialize the beginning of the massive injustice of slavery that's still playing out. We need this remembrance not for guilt or punishment, but to uproot the patterns of our national childhood.

❖ I used to think that nationalism was the only game in town. The most radical act was to support poor and formerly colonized countries in their right to be as nationalistic and boundary-obsessed as rich ones. Now I look at artificial boundaries—lines that can stop no current of air or drought or polluted river—and mourn the violence lavished on defending them. Long ago, in times suspiciously set aside as "prehistory," we were mostly nomadic peoples who claimed nothing but crisscrossing migratory paths. Cultures were the richest where different peoples and paths were most intermingled. We're still a nomadic species; indeed, we move and travel on this earth more than ever before. Yet we insist on the destructive fiction of nationalism, one that becomes even more dangerous when it joins with religions that try to create nationalistic gods.

As a group who can never afford the expensive fiction of having a nation—and whose bodies suffer from nationalism by being used as its means of reproduction—women of all races and cultures may be the most motivated to ask: How can we create a future beyond nationalism? After all, it has been around for less than five percent of humanity's history. We know we have had more migratory and communal ways of sharing this Spaceship Earth. There could be again.

If all this seems too impractical, let me add one more that is just a habit of mind: I used to think I would be rewarded for good behavior. Therefore, if I wasn't understood, I must not be understandable; if I wasn't successful, I must try harder; if something was wrong, it was my fault. More and more now, I see that context is all. When someone judges me or anyone or anything, I ask: *Compared to what?* When I see on television a series about children of divorce, for instance, I find myself asking: *What about a series on children of marriage?* When a woman fears the punishment that comes from calling herself a feminist, I ask: *Will you be so unpunished if you don't?* When I fear conflict and condemnation for acting a certain way, I think: *What peace or praise would I get if I didn't?*

I recommend the freedom that comes from asking: *Compared to what?* Hierarchical systems prevail by making us feel inadequate and imperfect. Whatever we do, we will internalize the blame. But once we realize there is no such thing as adequacy or perfection, it sets us free to say: *We might as well be who we really are.*

I realize in retrospect that fifty felt like leaving a much-beloved and familiar country—hence both the defiance and the sadness—and sixty felt like arriving at the border of a new one. I'm looking forward to trading moderation for excess, defiance for openness, and planning for the unknown. I already have one new benefit of this longer view:

I've always had two or more tracks running in my head. The pleasurable one was thinking forward to some future scene, imagining what should be, planning on the edge of fantasy. The other played underneath with all too realistic fragments of what I actually did or should have done in the immediate past. There it was in perfect microcosm, the past and future coming together to squeeze out the present—which is the only time in which we can be fully alive.

The blessing of what I think of as the last third of life (since I plan to reach a hundred) is that these past and future tracks have gradually dimmed until they are rarely heard.

More and more, there is only the full, glorious, alive-in-the-moment, don't-give-a-damn-yet-caring-for-everything sense of the right now.

I was about to end this with, *There's no second like the next one, I can't wait to see what happens*—which remains true. But this new state of mind would have none of it: *There's no second like this one.*

notes

i. *Memento Mori*, Muriel Spark, *New Directions Classic: New York*, page 153.

1. Barbara Macdonald, "Politics of Aging: I'm Not Your Mother." *Ms.* July/August 1990, p. 56.

2. Germaine Greer, *The Change: Women, Aging and the Menopause* (New York: Alfred A. Knopf, 1992), pp. 8, 387.

3. Paula Ries and Anne J. Stone, *The American Women 1992–93: A Status Report* (New York: W.W. Norton, 1992), p. 212. "The 21st Century family," Winter/Spring 1990 special issue of *Newsweek*, pp. 24, 63.

4. Barbara Macdonald with Cynthia Rich, *Look me in the Eye: Old Women, Aging and Ageism* (Minneapolis: Spinsters Ink, 1991).

5. James E. Birren, "The Process of Aging: Growing Up and Growing Old," in Alan Pifer and Lydia Bronte, eds., *Our Aging Society: Paradox and Promise* (New York: W.W. Norton, 1986), p. 267.

6. Gloria Steinem, "I Was a Playboy Bunny," in *Outrageous Acts and Everyday Rebellions* (New York: Holt, Rinehart & Winston, 1983), pp. 29-69.

7. The Schlesinger Library at Radcliffe College, 10 Garden Street, Cambridge, MA 02138; 617.495.8647. For a sampling, see *Letters to Ms. 1972–1987*, ed. Mary Thom (New York: Henry Holt, 1987).

8. Gloria Steinem, *Revolution from Within* (New York: Little, Brown, 1992).

9. Patricia J. Williams, *The Alchemy of Race and Rights* (Cambridge, Mass.: Harvard University Press, 1991), p. 216.

10. Audre Lorde, "Prologue", in *Undersong: Chosen Poems Old and New* (New York: W.W. Norton, 1992).

11. Carolyn Heilbrun, *Writing a Woman's Life* (New York: Ballantine Books, 1988), p. 123.

12. Gloria Steinem, "The Good News Is: These Are *Not* the Best Years of Your Life, " *Ms.*, September 1979, p. 64. Republished as "Why Young Women Are More Conservative," in *Outrageous Acts and Everyday Rebellions,* pp. 211-18.

13. M.N. Roy, *The Russian Revolution* (Calcutta: renaissance Publishers, 1949), p. x.

14. Gandhi's response to a reader in *Hind Swaraj,* a newspaper of which he was editor, quoted in *The Collected Works of Mahatma Gandhi* (New Delhi: Government of India, 1958–1984), vol. 10, p. 43.

15. Anne Koedt, "The Myth of the Vaginal Orgasm," reprinted in *Radical Feminism*, ed. Anne Koedt, Ellen Levine, and Anita Rapone (New York: Quadrangle Books, 1973), pp. 198-207.

16. To contact the once coordinator of these grassroots groups, write activist and parliament member, Nirmala Deshpande, Gandhi Ashram-Kingsway Camp. New Delhi, India; +91 11 27434514; nirmaladeshpande@gartindia.org.

17. A group dedicated to improving the legal, social, and economic conditions of people with disabilities so they may achieve complete integration into society. Contact the New York group to find or start groups in your area: Disabled In Action, Post Office Box 30954, Port Authority Station, New York, New York 10011–0109; 718.261.3737; www.disabledinaction.org.

18. *Black Women in America: An Historical Encyclopedia*, vol. 1, ed. Darlene Clark Hine (Brooklyn, N.Y.: Carlson Publishing, Inc., 1993), p. 93.

19. For a profile of Mary Peabody written by her granddaughter, Pulitzer Prize-winning author Frances Fitzgerald, see "My Most Unforgettable Character," *Reader's Digest*, September 1965.

20. Carrie Allen McCray, "Nobody Wrote a Poem," in *Piece of Time* (Goshen, Conn.: A Crimson Edge Chapbook of Chicory Blue Press with a special commitment to publishing women who began their major creative work after forty-five. For an anthology of twelve such women, edited by Sondra Zeidenstein and published by Chicory Blue in 1988, see *A Wider Giving: Women Writing After a Long Silence*.

21. United Seniors' Health Cooperative, 1331 H Street N.W., Suite 500, Washington, D.C. 20005; 202.393.6222; fax 202.783.0588.

22. Devaki Jain, "Remembering Kamaladevi," *Indian Express*, March 11, 1988.

23. For those who would like to continue a feminist Seder, see the *Women's Haggadah,* by E.M. Broner and Naomi Nimrod, plus the author's personal account of our experiences, in E.M. Broner, *The Telling* (San Francisco: HarperCollins, 1993).

elders academy press

What if we couldn't wait to be old, like a child can't wait to be an adult?"

Nader R. Shabahangi, Ph.D.

Through partnership with writers, Elders Academy Press seeks to encourage us to approach the process of aging with heightened awareness and to direct our thinking toward the possibilities ahead. The Press also seeks to help change cultural perceptions of the elderly and aging, which tend to largely focus on the negative.

Elders Academy Press was established in 2002 and is a program and publishing house of Pacific Institute and Pacific Institute Europe—both nonprofit organizations.

Based in San Francisco, Pacific Institute teaches new perspectives on aging in the field of gerontology and aims to reestablish the role of wisdom and eldership in our society. The Institute, founded in 1992,raises individual awareness, promotes social transformation, and helps advance, disseminate, and preserve knowledge in gerontological fields that focus on clinical, educational and human services purposes.

For more information about Pacific Institute and the publications of Elders Academy Press, please visit www.pacificinstitute.org or www.elderspress.org.

Titles published by Elders Academy Press are available at your local bookstore, online at www.amazon.com, online at www.elderspress.org or by calling 415.861.3455.

about the author

Gloria Steinem remains the United States' most influential, eloquent and revered feminist more than three decades after founding *Ms.* magazine. A devoted activist and writer, Steinem continues, as she has for most of her life, to travel nationally and internationally and speak with a calm voice of reason and articulation about gender, racial and other civil inequity issues.

Born in 1934 in Toledo, Ohio, she graduated from Smith College in 1956 and spent the following two years in India on a research fellowship. Her education in India would prove instrumental to her development as an activist and writer. Upon her return, she worked for her own research service and from 1960 worked as a freelance journalist. She often felt frustrated with the type of assignments she was given—"fluff assignments" reserved for "girl" journalists.

In 1968, she became the Contributing Editor and Political Editor of *New York Magazine* which she helped to found. During the 1960s, she emerged as a leading figure in the New Women's Movement in the United States and was also involved in other radical protest campaigns, particularly against the Vietnam War and against racism; she was Treasurer of the Committee for the Legal Defense of Angela Davis, and a firm supporter of crusading politicians such as Shirley Chisholm. In 1970, she was a co-founder of the Women's Action Alliance and the following year she convened the National Women's Political Caucus and co-founded *Ms.* magazine as a supplement to *New York Magazine.* It went solo in 1972 and within a year had reached a circulation of 350,000. Many of Steinem's essays have been collected and published as books.

Steinem became a spokesperson for issues about aging quite accidentally after declaring to a reporter on the occasion of her fortieth birthday, "This is what forty looks like. We've been lying for so long, who would know?" After this unintentional proclamation about what forty looked like for her and about the collective societal "pressure to 'pass' by lying about one's age," Steinem received so many words of thanks and so many observations from other women facing age bias that she began to truly realize the profundity and dimension of age oppression.

In her inspiring essay "Doing Sixty," Steinem described turning fifty as "leaving a much-beloved and familiar country" and turning sixty "as arriving at the border of a new one" in which she looked forward to "trading moderation for excess, defiance for openness, and planning for the unknown.

The deaths of friends and colleagues and her husband, activist David Bale, have profoundly affected Steinem. Of David, she says "both his presence in my life and his absence resulted in a shift in the way I see other people and what I assume about relationships."

When recently asked by a journalist how turning seventy had been unlike turning fifty or sixty, Steinem's answer was stunning in its simplistic universality. "It is different because it has a ring of mortality— so it has a big message of stop wasting time."

Has Gloria Steinem ever wasted time? By most accounts, she has been busily changing the world for the better.

other titles by elders academy press

AgeSong: Meditations for Our Later Years
Elizabeth Bugental, Ph.D.

Growing old is not an option. But how we age is a choice. At least we like to think so. *AgeSong* gives us a pleasurable nudge and a little inspiration to take charge of our aging. None of us knows how many years this final life-phase will last, but it's a pretty good bet that it will last at least as long as our adolescence. If we can remember back that far, unlike this life-phase, those teens and early twenties seemed to go on forever and we sure didn't have a plan. Now we're old enough and maybe even wise enough to decide how we'd like to live before we die. And maybe we even have the guts to make the choices we need to make to do it in style.

AgeSong can be taken in small doses to direct our thinking toward the possibilities ahead of us rather than the life we've left behind. It provides us a simple, yet profound, breathing space to take in the richness within our reach that could fill our last days with wonder and gratitude.

Elizabeth Bugental spent her 20s and 30s as a Catholic nun in Los Angeles. She has taught on all levels and was, for over a decade, Chairperson of the Department of Theatre Arts at Immaculate Heart College in Los Angeles. Her second career was as a psychotherapist in the San Francisco Bay Area, in private practice and working jointly with her husband of thirty-six years, James Bugental, notes psychologist and author. Elizabeth holds a doctorate in Speech and Drama from Stanford University and a master's degree from Catholic University of America.

other titles by elders academy press

Faces of Aging
Nader Robert Shabahangi, Ph.D.

Faces of Aging is a collection of photographs and essays that address the challenges of aging in a society that is not sympathetic to older people. The result of this negativity deprives us all from interaction with a very valuable segment of the population.

Older people can provide us with experience, knowledge and friendship if we change or attitude toward them and begin to see them as a resource rather than a liability. History and the humanistic tradition have shown us that when respected and valued older citizens can continue to be productive and creative and can contribute to the quality of life.

Faces of Aging is a tribute to elders and is dedicated to removing the veil from the subject of aging. The book invites us to ask how we can remain conscious of the ways in which we impose our own fears of aging, of death, of the changes that invariably occur as we age, onto the elderly themselves: If we ask ourselves to face our own fears of aging and dying, maybe we can begin to understand how these fears express themselves in our interaction with and attitudes toward the elderly.

Nader received his doctorate from Stanford University researching basic philosophical assumptions underlying present-day psychotherapies. He has worked extensively with elders for more than ten years.

other titles by elders academy press

The Therapies of Literature
Richard Wiseman, Ph.D.

The Therapies of Literature is a tour de force of the finest works of world literature. This book helps readers face the central questions awareness-seeking humans ask: Are we fulfilling our life contract? Are we living the life we meant to live? It reaches out to readers in all of their amazing diversity, depth and richness.

As notes by Rollo May in the foreword, "the author has been capable of presenting the book as a completely new way of conceptualizing human life, its meaning and purpose, which will ultimately have to stand behind all psychotherapists' efforts to be helpful to their fellow humans."

Dr. Wiseman received his doctorate in literature from the University of California, Berkeley, with postdoctoral study and research at the Sorbonne, Paris, the Thomas Mann Archives and the C.G. Jung Institute in Zürich. He later received an M.A. in Psychology at the Professional School of Psychology in San Francisco. He taught at several schools, including U.C. Berkeley and San Francisco State University where he was Professor of Foreign Languages and Literatures as well as Department Chair of World and Comparative Literature.

other titles by elders academy press

Caregiving from the Heart: Tales of Inspiration
Riki Intner, M.A. and Roberta Cole, M.A.

Throughout *Caregiving from the Heart* are stories of true experience. We hear from children, friends, relatives and partners, long distance caregivers and many recipients of care. The shared stories help us to navigate the maze of emotion that can be at once tearful and ebullient, gut wrenching and heartwarming. The stories cover moments large and small and often address elder issues of pressing concern—from depression to loss of mobility and even to last chance romance. We learn that there is no right way to care and that caregiving opens windows on the full range of possibility available to us when we participate in one of the most profound adventures of our lives. The stories speak of agony and surprise—of joy and despair—but most of all, of discovery. *Caregiving from the Heart* is like having a support group in your own home.

Roberta Cole is a communications professional. She has hosted and produced programs for WNBC and WYNY radio as well as WNYC, the flagship station of National Public Radio. She currently teaches at New York University and lives in New York with her husband and daughter.

Riki Intner is a Marriage and Family Therapist. She lives in San Francisco, California with her husband after raising three children who now have children of their own. She has been in private practice for over twenty years and has also conducted workshops and training sessions at conferences, schools, businesses and community events. She has proudly served on the board of her chapter and district Rotary Clubs. She is a Diplomate in Adlerian Psychology.